Dancing in the Rain

~ struggles
~ reflections
~ triumphs

Kaltrina Hoti

Copyright © 2021 by Kaltrina Hoti, Kathleen Collins.
All rights reserved.

Published by Diamond Publishing Company

All characters and events in this book are fictitious.
All resemblances to persons, living or dead, are
purely coincidental.

No part of this document may be reproduced or
transmitted in any form or by any means, electronic,
mechanical, photocopying, recording, or otherwise,
without prior written permission of Diamond Publishing
Comany.

For information regarding permission, or book club/bulk
order pricing write to Diamond Publishing Company
28 S. Oak St., La Crescent, MN 55947
Attention: Katy

ISBN: 978-1-944906-06-1
Printed in the U.S.A.
1st Edition

Contents

Dancing in the Rain 1
Today 2
Time 3
Her Tree 4
I Miss You 5
My Moon 6
On The Corner Of The Street 7
When 8
I Love You From A Distance 9
The End Of The Beginning 10
Fourteen Days 11
Giving Tears 14
Studio 15
Can I Change Time? 17
Selfish That You Are 18
Untold Story 19
One More Time 20
The Other Side 22
The End Of The Day 23
Come With Me 24
Don't Cry 25
I'm Ready Now 26
I Was So Pure 27
I Meet Hendry 28
How Far Do We Want To Go? 30

Contents

Inside Of Me 31
Salvatore Is His Name. 32
Peace Of Christmas Eve 33
I Cried Yesterday. 34
You Can't Be Forgotten. 35
I'm Reaching For You 36
Between Us. 37
You Want Me To Be Gone 39
My Supporter. 40
Your Face 41
I Was In Deep Sleep 42
Nobody. 44
Don't Look Back 45
Hold My Hand. 46
Because Of Mountain Days 47
Saranda. 48
Linda's Eyes 49
Grandpa, Tell Me A Story. 50
I Don't Want To Leave You. 52
Golden Coins Took My Friend 54
Beautiful Night 55
He Dreamed. 56
I Wish I Stopped 57
If You Let Me 58
Word Of God. 59

Contents

Dean Smith.. 60
New Beginning 61
Old Friendship.. 62
I Asked God 63
The Inside Of My Day....................................... 64
Power Of Purple Color...................................... 65
True Words... 66
Did You Remember 67
Our Melodies... 68
Panorama Of Studio 69
What Happened?... 70
Butterfly 71
Moment 72
Stolen Moment.. 73
After The Rain 74
I Miss My Father... 75
Dream.. 76
Tattooed Face.. 77
Over The Rainbow 78
For The First Time... 80
My Brush 81
In The Red Book 82

Dedication

⌘

This book is dedicated to the power that creates beauty in each of us, and then we, through words, connect our minds with our emotions and give, and present our moment in time to others.

Through these poems we want to remind ourselves:

*"Every question has an answer.
What we do with an answer is the question."*

A Note from the Author

⌘

Dear Readers,

Thank you for taking time to dance through the rain with me. Writing and painting are my heart and soul's biggest weapons for not just surviving, but thriving in God's goodness.

Some of the poems in this book I can't even consider to be mine. Yes, I wrote them; they were in my mind, but they felt also like messages for you. You will know which poems are yours.

When we are experiencing the biggest challenges of life, a mere word can lift us up and turn us into survivors; likewise, it takes only one word to drag us down into dark colors where we can't see, with no hope beyond our faith.

But we carry inside us more s t r e n g t h than we realize when we refuse to accept moments of regret, for none of us are perfect.

The beauty of reading poems is that everybody finds their own connection within them. It will delight me if my words make you feel free and happy.

Each of you has a poem inside of your heart. From time to time, stop and try to write it down.

I wrote my first poem when I was ten years old. Amazingly, I still have it. For me, writing poems means painting the canvas with words instead of colors.

Everything we create—art, music, stories, poems—has a purpose. To share that with others is the only way we can stay connected inside the culture.

Thank you for considering this book. It is written for you. Enjoy reading the poems; I think you will find a shadow of yourself within.

My respect to the readers,

Kaltrina Hoti

Dancing In The Rain

⌘

It was one of those warm, spring rains.
The sky was alive with red and purple colors.
I was walking through green grass that was thirsty for drops of clouds.
I opened my arms; they felt like feathers.

It was one of those warm, spring rains. I reached for the sky.
My arms turn into wings,
And I danced with the sun.
God washed my face, kissed my eyes.
I was dancing with rain while wind was making love between us.

It was one of those warm, spring rains that you wish you could kiss.
It was the rain of love that comes when you love every moment of your life.
I was dancing in one of those warm, spring rains,
Waiting to see who else would come to touch open sky.
Dancing in the rain is loving life.

Today

⌘

Today, I felt the eyes of a little girl, touching my heart so deeply
Those eyes
Are the eyes of my little girl
She is so special in so many different ways.
I remember the moments when I prayed to God for her,
And she became my lifetime gift full of the love I needed.
Through her, I met God, and received hope and faith.

Today, the eyes of the little girl touched my heart.
My little girl,
She received *her* gift from God, and gave me tears of happiness.
You can cry them only one time in life.
My girl gave birth of new life today.
I felt life, with tears of happiness.

Today, I felt the eyes of a little girl touching my heart so deeply.
They opened a new window of my life.

Time

⌘

Time is aware of my life; there is so much time left,
And I have not seen anything yet.
You may miss me and wonder... *What happened to her?*
If you see those magic colors in the sky,
That is me
Making my life for me and what I was meant to be.
Alive, in the moment when seasons are changing their nature
Alive, in the moment when the sky is creating rain.
Alive for my story, alive for my soul.
That woman walking with the light around her
Reaching for the stars at night,
That woman is me.
You've never seen me like this before.
It's time for you to listen to me and see what is hiding inside of me.
Time is aware of my life. I am learning to smile and live.

Her Tree

⌘

She runs and lies down under the shadow of her tree,
Closes her eyes, and dreams her dream.

Dreams are magical and real. They all come true
If you learn to wait, knowing they are on the way.
The wind is kissing her face. She kisses the wind back.
Is that possible?

Dreams are magical and true. Yes, you can hug the wind back.
She runs to her tree, lies under its shadow,
And dreams her dream.
She just begins her first step
Of giving part of her to the world.
Her dream is hope of her vision, faith in her story.

Dreams are magical and true.
Keep dreaming under the shadow of your tree.

I Miss You

⌘

One tear is for your eyes and smile that I am going to miss.
A deep breath is for the words that we exchange in so many different ways.
It's like part of my body is pulling away from me.
One tear is for me; I am going to miss you every moment of your life.
Some things God creates will never be understood. This feeling is one of them.
Loving a child is a mystery of life.

Giving tough love is learning to live for me and you.
Take your passion and desire of your life in your hands.
I will be waiting for you to wipe tears from my face.
Tough love is learning to live life for me and you.
They say the mother is like a candle.
She burns her emotion to give light to her child.
I hope you see my light that I am trying to give you.
One tear is for the red rose that is waiting for you.

My Moon

⌘

My eyes are full of tears.
I can only show them to the moon light
That is covering me tonight.
I am talking to the stars and purple sky
Now that everything from the day is silenced,
Listen to my voice.

I am sharing my heart and searching for the answer
That is blessed from the stars and the wisdom of the moonlight.

I am looking for a place to cry where nobody can know me or
   see me.
My eyes are full of tears, but I don't want anybody to see them.

I am waiting for the light of moon to cover me and gently take
   me
Between the clouds so I can cry inside of me.
I am too weak for my heart, too strong for the outside world. I
   wear the crown on my head,
But tonight, I cry for the lost dream, trying to learn,
Where does this feeling end or begin?
Why do I have to suffer for love that doesn't know me?
   Why? Why? Why?
I am wishing for something that does not know I exist.
They say that every person in our lives comes and goes for a
   reason.
I can't wait to find out— where do you fit in my life?
Look inside my eyes. You will be surprised.

On The Corner Of The Street
⌘

A million pictures inside one moment,
A moment that belongs to you and me,
A moment that we created on the streets of New York.
Through my eyes, I am trying to see.
Who are you?
Why do you dress that way?
In your eyes, you are asking, "Why are you staring at me?"
We both have one thing in common:
An echo of that New York street that is whispering to us. You are a million pictures in one moment.
You can be me. I can be you.
Or you can be you and I can be me.
We can choose to take it as far as we want.
Inside of a million pictures, in one moment, inside the streets of New York,
We ask, we wonder, we wish, we wait.
We dream, and in the end, we become the echo of the New York street.
A million pictures in one moment. You, me, and them, in the streets of New York City,
Where everything is alive before the beginnings of new stories that will come.

When
⌘

You just never know when the light will shine over you.
You just never know when the breeze of wind will swipe you
From the present moment
and take you in wonder, where you have to find out why you are
   there.

You just never know where your beginning or ending is
Of the story you think you created.
It is like becoming part of that rock on the side of the road. It is
   like becoming a letter of a big sign
That divides south from west, north from east.
It is like melting words from somebody's dream. You just never
   know which side of life you will take
'Til you let the moment go through your vision and it whispers,
   "It is the right time and moment."
You just don't know where and why you become part of the
   light
That, believe it or not, belongs to you.

I Love You From A Distance

⌘

With the tips of my fingers, I am touching your skin.
I close my eyes to feel this moment through my imagination.
Invisible, I reach for your lips. You are wondering
What is happening around you?
You feel love, not knowing from where!
It's me. I am loving you from a distance,
Because that's all you gave me.
To me, you are an undreamed dream.
To you, I'm just a shadow that you can't see.
But today, I'm loving you from a distance.
Through your hair, my fingers are playing.
Closer and closer, our bodies are melting in one.
You are wondering what is happening around you.
I am dreaming an undreamed dream in the light of the day,
Taking what my heart is crying for and what belongs to me.
While you are wondering how you can feel an invisible touch,
I am taking every drop of you away from me, forever.
Can you cry without tears?

The End Of The Beginning

⌘

Stop for moment. Just listen.
Let your angel on the right shoulder tell you a story
About you… and show you what the light of love
Can do for the world that you are in.
Stop and listen for just a moment.
Give your mind and heart a challenge.
Do you think you can touch invisible? Yes, you can.
If you let your heart read the world,
Everything is there for you.
Everything in our lives is gathered in one place, one very small place,
But the power is so big.
There is nothing you can't be or do. Let your heart read the world.
That is the only way to see the power. That is the only way you can learn
To feel what you breathe and what you touch,
And when you cry for the first time,
You just begin to live through the power over yourself,
The end of the beginning just beginning.

Fourteen Days

⌘

That day. In silence, I said goodbye
To my childhood, my friends and family,
And started walking on an unknown road.
Not because I wanted to, but because I was still thirsty for life
   and dreams.

The first day, I was crying together with the rain, so nobody
   would know
I was washing away my past.
I didn't have space in my heart to keep anything anymore,
But I still could smell the fresh paint of the living room
That summer you painted the house, Mother.

The second day, I danced with the wind, trying to reach
For a new beginning. I didn't even know what to expect.
It was so hard to fight with present time.
I had too many dreams I built before I realized I had to let
   them go,
Not because I wanted to, but because I was still thirsty for life
   and dreams.

The third day, I talked to the moon, asking him to shine over me
So darkness wouldn't take me in fear.
There were days of hunger and thirst.
The funny part was, I did not want water or bread.
I just wanted to see the other side of the fence.

The fourth day, I was telling a story to the stars,
One more time giving me hope and faith for the unknown road
That I am walking right now.
It seemed each hour was a year, each day was a lifetime.

For the first time, if I could watch the sun go down,
It was the accomplishment of the day.

The fifth day, I prayed for my father to hear my voice. I was
    breathing with my last strength of hope.
Time was lost.
People became just figures.
I needed a miracle to happen.

The sixth day, I let my angels take me away and lead me
Over the big mountain;
I knew I couldn't do it alone.
My prayer was answered, and for the first time,
I felt God was watching me.

The seventh day, I heard a storm calling my name.
I am still walking through an unknown road.
This time, I am stronger than in the beginning.
He touched me, gave me a smile. I knew what time it was.

The eighth day, I called on the moon, the stars, and the rain to
    give me my soul back. I was not crying anymore.
I just needed one more day to watch the sun hiding behind the
    mount.

The ninth day, I slept with rocks in the wild forest.
The blue sky covered me. I heard voices that loved me.

The tenth day, I was covered with morning dew.
Together with the red roses, I opened the door for another day.

By the time the eleventh day came, I was thanking
The blue sky for the miracles of life.

On the twelfth day, I was thinking, "We think we can plan our lives in advance, but there is so much to learn."

The thirteenth day, I cried again. This time, I let everybody see my tears.
I was almost on the other side of fence,
Tired and thirsty and hungry.

On the fourteenth day, I let my Father, God, wipe my tears.
I am there, walking on the road that knows me well.

Everything around us knows us before we know them.
I learned in fourteen days I can live my life. Life can't live my life.

Giving Tears

⌘

You teach us not to cry because we are Your children.
You teach us to keep trying 'til the last breath,
With the hope and faith that
You gave us.
Today, I am crying
The tears of past.
Everything is washing off.
I see the open doors for happiness in her life.
Today, I am crying because
You gave me the tears
To wash my soul from the past.
You tell us to walk together with You.
From time to time,
You will let us cry
For them
When we see the doors of happiness in their lives.
Giving tears from You,
A spark of the light that is us.
Today, I am crying for the first time.

Studio

⌘

It feels so good, it's been part of my daily birth.
Inside of the new song, a new story on the canvas
Has been part of that morning light that wakes up the easel
   every day.

I like to do things I can't do until I learn to do them well.

He sits on his chair by the window and watches every morning.
The light of the sun slowly shines over the canvas with the music
Of yesterday's story. He tries to breathe lightly so he can feel the
   music
When the light of the sun takes him inside the canvas.

I like to do things I can't do until I learn to do them well.

Today, he remembered an old wish he had, sixty-five years ago.
Inside his favorite brush, there is an untold story to tell.
It felt good becoming part of his story, where I was the first one
To hear the story; another birth of art is born.

I like to do things I can't do until I learn to do them well.

It feels so good to be part of a daily birth
Inside of the new song, the new story on the canvas,
Being part of that morning light that wakes up the easel every
   day.
From time to time, you ask yourself, do you feel what is happen-
   ing?

I like to do things I can't do until I learn to do them well.

Something different is happening today. Will I understand this?
He is holding his brush in one hand. He did not hear my steps
Coming inside between the studio silence and his easel.
Finally, our eyes create a connection with the moment.
I will never forget the words he spoke to me.
It is time for me to tell a story to my canvas and my brushes,
And one day, I may tell you what it was!

I need you to live.
For how long, I don't know.
My story is too short and too long.

I like to do things I can't do until I learn to do them well.

Waiting for him to tell his story.
Will I do well on waiting?
I hope.

Can I Change Time?

⌘

No words inside of me...I want to bring past time back
And take my pain away from where it began.
No words inside of me...I want to change the time
And teach myself how to love my own heart.

No words inside of me...I am trying to feel the world around
   me.
It is not real or moving because there are no words inside of me.
I want to change the time
Before I start crying my words I can't find.

Can I change time?
I looked up in the deep sky, asking for my answer. Something
   touched my face...It felt like love.
Even today, I still don't know for sure.

It felt like my shadow touched me, to wake me up
From a deep sleep; a soft voice was talking to me,
"You can change time with a life full of love and smiles.
The one who took your words before,
Make them the past.
You can choose your new words from inside of this night."

Can I change time? I will call my name with smiles and love.
Can I change time? No, I don't want to.
This time,
Time can mold me.

Selfish That You Are

⌘

Again, it is happening. I bring myself to the edge of life
And think, *what now?*
You are taking my pride and expect me to still smile back.
So selfish that you are, you can't see your faces in mirrors,
But I forgive you.
I am stronger than you in every way you can think of.
I am me and what I believe; you are fire between the lines of truth.
You know the sound and feeling of it, but you choose to ignore it.
But the truth will never ignore you.
I am stronger than you in every way you can think of.
I am the smile from a strange child; I am the tear of a grown man.
You are so selfish you can't recognize your father's voice,
But you can hear the words:
"My son, don't let the truth run after you. One day, you will be alone."
You are so selfish you can't see your face in the mirror,
But I forgive you.
My friend, our lives will cross somewhere again.

Untold Story

⌘

Drink the morning dew from her lips.
Still thirsty for some more,
My fingers play atop her silky skin.
The light in her eyes is drawing me in to search
For secret thoughts inside the untouched soul of hers.
On the pillow, her golden hair is shining;
I am scared to touch it.
It reminds me of the first sunlight in the morning
That hides the story of yesterday.
I drink the morning dew from her lips, still thirsty for more.
Can I stop the time and feel this moment 'til I get lost inside her beauty?
To make love, it takes two. To tell a love story, it takes only one person.
The man is wishing his story never to be told.

One More Time

⌘

Before the day began, I was on the road.
In front of me are ten hours of driving,
But I can't feel this distance. In my mind, it is just around the corner.
As the sun started shining, I was following the light
Where she is waiting for me.

One more time to hug her and say hello and goodbye in the same time.

I walk slowly, watching every face I see.
Everybody looks the same.
For the first time, I see through to the inside of my heart instead of using my eyes.
I am still searching for my girl, scared but thirsty to touch her face.
I saw her from a distance. She was looking around.
My steps were faster.
I am finally in front of her, looking her in the eyes before I take her in my arms.
One more time to hug her and say hello and goodbye in the same time.
They told us we could hug and kiss them now, but when we walk with them in the streets,
They are mirrors of them,
Just shadows of us. They will be walking strength and proud to be Army,
And we can be part of that as we watch them and remember that.
One more hug we gave them and said hello and goodbye to them in the same time.
I heard her voice from inside talking to me...

Mom, I am a soldier. Meet my family. And I cried without tears.
I smiled and was happy to see her new vision and new family. I keep forever my moment when I...
One more time, I hugged her and said hello and goodbye in the same time.
This is going to keep me alive, this moment of new beginning,
A new ending for the old dreams that we have known through history,
Of the flag and the voice of freedom.
My child chose to become one of the stars
Of our most powerful flag in the world...she is Army today.

God saw my tears and the love that I had for my girl.
He told my girl, "One more time, lay your head in your mother's lap.
She wants to feel you one more time
Before she hugs you and says hello and goodbye
   in the same time."

Soldiers are under one name, one family, with justice as their vision.
I love you, my girl...I will walk the same way you are, proud with challenge.

The Other Side
⌘

We feel, we dream, we want, we wish.
All this keeps us connected with the other side
Where the mystery of our lives is hiding.
When is the right time
To grab the moment that ballooned to us?
How do we know which flower bloomed just for my eyes?
When do you know to say…*I love*…for the first time?
When you give everything you have for the dream inside
Of your spirit, but the window is not open yet,
Do you still fight for it?
When do you know it is time to change the path?
Listen to the voice inside of you. That is the other side
Teaching you to tear the tears between the sun and the rain,
Showing you how to name your own stars,
Inviting you to catch the first morning dew,
Showing you there are more colors you can wish to see
Inside the rainbow.
Listen to the truth inside of you, which is the other side,
That we all wonder to see.

The End Of The Day

⌘

Yellow is the old cat of mine.
At the end of the day,
He lies in a circle inside the chair next to me.
He breathes so deep and slow, and from time to time,
He will open his eyes to make sure I am still there.
But Tic Tack is under my feet playing with my toes,
Pulling my socks off; he is full of energy even
   at the end of the day.
Funny thing about him is that during the day, he will
   not come to me—
He will pass me, not even think I am there, but in the evening,
   He is under my feet, playing and trying to be closer to me.
Yellow will grouch from time to time.
My old, yellow cat is a wise friend of mine.
Tic Tack is cute and full of energy and the love of meow world.
At the end of the day, we are in the circle watching the sunset.

Kaltrina Hoti

Come With Me
⌘

Here is a river with magic rocks that shine through the water
With colors you've never seen before, and if you take a rock
In your hand, it will glow and turn into a dragonfly.
You can walk barefoot inside the river and be whatever you
  wish.
If you swim, golden fish will take you inside the heart of the
  river ,
Where another world is waiting to open your heart
  and give you
Unseen, untouched love.
If you drink river water, it washes your pain away.

You will take a deep breath and feel pure like a pearl inside the
  shell.
You can stand on the old rock and watch your face reflecting
Inside the river, showing you the beauty of your soul.
Come with me. I want to show you my secret place.

When the sun goes to hide, the last shining light
  opens the river.
You can see angels dancing together before the night begins
To call the stars and ask the moon to smile over us.
Come with me, just for one night, to share a moment
That I wish you to have.
Come with me before somebody
Steals the magic from the rocks.
Come with me to see the open sky.
Come with me, my love.

Don't Cry

⌘

Inside of your eyes is the ocean where we left our footprints.
Remember that long walk on the beach that we shared every night?
Don't cry for me when I am going…
You will wash off the footprints of our love.
I need your heart to smile all the time because sadness will
    Bring rain over our footprints of love…I need you to smile all the time
So I can live inside of your eyes.
I will be the wind that plays with your hair to remind you to smile for me all the time…don't cry when I am gone. I will send the bird to sing a song just for you.
I will turn into morning dew…when you pick your favorite flower,
I will be kissing you…don't cry for me when I am gone. Inside of your eyes, there is the sparkle of light.
It will lead you to me when the time is right.
Don't cry for me when I am gone…where I am going is peace and love. The sparkle in your eyes will find
Me again, my darling, angel face.

I Am Ready Now

✤

I was inside the wind, listening for every movement from every
    corner,
And then, from nowhere, everything stopped.
The wind took me back to where the beginning was.
Everything was still.
I was able to hear silence inside my voice.
It scared me for second. I could see myself between everything.
I felt I could touch deep into the sky and the dark night.
Is this my learning time?
I am here not by accident. I know something from this moment.
I have to take it with me. Oh, now I see.
When everything around you is challenging, smile.
You are becoming stronger. Only through pain
    will you know love.
Only through darkness can you see light.
I am ready to go. Wind, take me back to where
    I stumbled my time.
I am ready now to become stronger in my mind.

I Was So Pure

⌘

From time to time I think of the past.
I want to feel again the first innocent kiss I gave you. I was so pure then. Passion and love lived inside of me.
I was ready to give you my dreams and wishes,
But you poisoned everything I hoped for.
You put the big stone in my soul. I still wonder,
Will I ever be loved again?
From time to time, I think of the past,
Wishing that time was just a dream, hoping I will wake up
And see the world through innocent eyes again.
I was so pure then. I didn't know how life could be better. You gave me my first bite to taste sadness
I wonder if you know; you owe me a life story.
You took from me everything I loved after I gave you
My first innocent kiss.
I still wonder, *Can I trust in love again?*

I meet Hendry

⌘

When I met him for the first time, my heart and mind
Went in two directions at the same time.
We opened our friendship by shaking with our left hands.
I was listening deeply to his words.
I wanted to know more of him before I said anything.
He was wearing a yellow sweater.
The sleeve of the right arm was pinned on his shoulder.
Hendry had one arm only.
He was born with this challenge that affects the
 world of others.
He carries a smile on his face all time,
A smile that you can't see with your eyes, but with your heart...
When I met him the first time, my heart and mind went in two
 directions at the same time.
Was I supposed to feel sorry that Hendry had one arm?
Or did I just not look at the sleeve of the yellow sweater
 pinned to his shoulder?
But Hendry taught me to look at him like a man with two
 arms.
He asked me:
"Can you tie your shoe with one hand?" I never tried, my friend.
He sat on a bench, and I watched. He untied his shoes and then
 tied them back up with one hand only.
He looked at me with his special smile and said, "When I was
 in the first grade, my mother taught me to do this.
She gave the wisdom of everyday life: To learn to survive and
 challenge myself,
To do anything around me like those with two arms. I played
 basketball and tennis, and I fished a lot.
I lived with two arms from the beginning.

I am like everybody else, asking God to be with me and fighting to have better dreams everyday." Today, I still shake our friendship with my left hand, but my mind and heart see him in one direction, with a strong spirit and a smile in his soul.

I see him as a man with two strong arms. I have a friend called handsome Hendry.

He received an Olympic medal playing tennis with one arm.

The power of God can't be massacred, but we can see it inside of each of us…when you feel sometimes sad, remember my friend Hendry who can tie his shoes

with one hand.

How Far Do We Want To Go?

⌘

We can be between the sky and earth.
We can talk with each other without saying a word. We compare
 our wisdom with the speed of light.
We can create friendships without shaking a hand. How far do
 we want to go?
To make our world an easy way to live,
They say time changes…is it with us or because of us? Maybe
 we will ask this question before it is not too late to understand
 we can change our habits
But not the nature of our lives.
The handshake of two people is power that can't be replaced;
 Words spoken from a bar room of our soul can build
A bridge between the possible and the impossible.
Time will change with us…if we let a stone sleep in his own
 water
And let the rain and the sky be connected through wind and
 stars, things that change because of us will die in us.
Things that change will us to open the window to became a part
 of that time.

Inside Of Me

⌘

There are so many words inside of me,
Hidden between questions and wonders that I have. I know
　everything in this life has answers and ways;
Finding them is a challenge between our hearts and minds.
　There are so many words inside of me,
Trapped in my heart and waiting to get free. I can feel them
　and they are troubling me.
I stare at stars in this quiet night, hoping they will open the
　window of my soul and show me the way.
How can I bring peace in my words so they can talk to me?
　And bring sparkly fire in my eyes?

Salvatore Is His Name

⌘

I love your eyes, the way they look at me
I like your smile, almost invisible, but so real…your words are from the heart with wisdom of the past
And a vision of future…you are the man who never cries. I admire your way of living in the past and fighting for the present with the last strength in you.
You are the man who never cries for the moments that we miss in our lives.
You sacrifice yourself, for promises you made. You wish everybody to be on top of their dreams.
You have so much passion for things you imagine. You create a future just by looking at the beauty of life. Your name is a spell of love and hope and faith.
You are the man who never cries…You are my best friend. Inside of your eyes, I see you lived time that never
will be repaid
And took the wisdom of that experience and turned it into present happiness.
Don't ever ask him a question unless you want to hear the truth.
If you need his help, it will be there before you realize it. In life, we all need comfort from another person.
This is a man who never cries…and he is part of my life. If I say I love, it is not enough.
If I say I need you, it isn't all I want to say.
This is the man who promises to you and me, and to time, to be faithful.
Salvatore is his name.

Peace Of Christmas Eve

⌘

It's Christmas Eve, and I am sitting outside on a chair on my porch
And listening to the peace of this night.
We celebrate His birth with the first sunshine that will come in the morning.
Some of us have Him in our hearts and let Him shine on our path of life.
Some of us don't even think of Him till this night The beauty of Him is
He loves us all the same, no matter what.
He gave His life for you and me, so that we could look at the enemy,
And with strength in our eyes, say, "It doesn't have to be this way."
If you hate another person, you're making scars in your life.
 Forgiveness is what He teaches us, because we are
made to make mistakes.
It's Christmas Eve, and I am listening to the peace of this night.
I can hear His voice
Forgive those who put tears in your eyes.
Open the door of love, even if others are pushing you away. You are never alone as long as I exist, and my light is forever. It's Christmas Eve, and I am sitting outside and talking to His light
That sleeps in my soul.

I Cried Yesterday

⌘

I cried yesterday from so deep within my heart.
I called for my father in heaven to help me with my pain. I cried so deeply from my heart and closed my eyes
While the tears washed my face.
And my voice tried to reach his power.
I cried and cried and cried till He told me
To use those tears to wash my pain away and let Him open a new door for the beginning of His way.
Last night, I cried and cried.
Today, I let Him open my new vision.
If you know you have been walking through His light tears will dry fast, and the fire of a new vision will open your smile to live with your own power
That He gave you a long time ago.
Yesterday I cried…today I am ready for a new beginning that He teaches me through my tears.
He is light after life and life after light.

You Can't Be Forgotten

✠

You can't be forgotten by Him…He knows everything and sees it all.
So when you're in pain, He will see you more. You can't be forgotten by Him;
He is there all the time,
You may not think of Him while you have everything your way
And you think you can do it all by yourself,
But when you lose your wordy world, He still waits for you, to show you it can happen again in a better way.
He can do what you thought never possible to happen. He is always watching us, and He is waiting for those who do not recognize Him, to show them the real way.
Of living life with full meaning of reason is why we are here. You are not forgotten…just open your mind and soul. When you think it is over, He will build a new way.
You can't be forgotten by Him…He loves you too much.

Kaltrina Hoti

I Am Reaching For You

⌘

I can't say I am sorry for the life that happened. We lived what was given to us.
You can't choose which battle you want to fight.
I don't want to say I am sorry for the tears that I cried. It's been a long time since I slept with both eyes closed. Let me dream for the first time.
Don't ask me to say I am sorry…don't tell me I was wrong.
You can't choose which battle you want to fight.
You take a deep breath of hope and faith and make the best of your soul trying to let the light of life shine on you always. I am reaching for you…come with me to the new challenges. Without the tears of the past, I am smiling inside of your eyes. Give me a shadow of our life back…
Don't tell me to say I am sorry
For tears that I cried…one day you will say the same thing.
My darling daughter, take my hand, let's walk together.

Between Us

⌘

It is heaviness, and I become a yellow leaf around you. The
thoughts and words that surround our world are gray.
I have to take a long walk away to bring the feeling of peace and
life back into me!
Do I make you a winner?
Do I let myself be your shadow?
My mind is fighting right now this moment.

I never took your moment from the stories you told me. I never
stepped on your emotions.
I tried to let light be there for you when you needed it. What
happened that you couldn't see that?
I am strong and full of love and forgiveness…so, even if I go
away,
I am doing it for my own light that is strong inside my soul, not
because you wish me to be gone.
I am saying to you…take whatever you thought you wanted to
have.

I forgive you for those ugly words you said; they are yours. They
deserve you…I will not reach for them…because I have so
much light inside my soul.
When I am gone, your darkness
Will become blind from the power of my light.
You will just be somebody who I will pray for all the time to
wake up and see there is another choice.

I am strong and full of love to continue another page of life.
You will be somebody I will always pray for to wake up. You
helped me to learn how to see the difference between darkness and light.

I am gone as a winner…you are in the same dark spot, and that is the difference between us.
One day, you will see what light can do over the darkness of life.
Light and darkness were between us.

You Want Me To Be Gone

⌘

The Christmas tree is wondering, where did I go?
The flowers are thirsty for my touch and untold stories. The sun is wondering where my shadow is.
Birds are looking to sing their songs to me, and you have to answer to all this.
What are you going to say?
I will be listening to you from a distance.
Do you know you have to have a candle to light darkness? Do you know that for a sunshiny day, a blue sky is needed?
Do you know by now that thirst can be replaced only with pure water?
Do you know you can only once walk through the path of life?
Think again what you are going to say. I will be listening from the distance.
Now you want me to be gone
Because you are scared of me and what I can do with my touch.

My Supporter
⌘

I shared with you so many moments, days, months, and years,
  Early in the mornings, late at night, talking about the stories
That I wanted the world to see as a part of me and you. It all
  begins with the color white
That you held in front of me as a mirror of my thoughts. It all
  begins with a white color,
Whiter than the first snow, whiter than a white cloud before it
  rains,
Whiter than the white hair of an old, wise man.
You know when my hand touches you and tries to wake you up,
  You are always happy to hear my voice, even when
I fight with my words.
You always stand still and hold the mirror of my thoughts until
  I find the answer of the right moment and color.
Through you, I blessed others in different ways and gave them
  visions of life.
Through you I kept the touch of an unforgotten history of man.
  Through you, my loyal friend, forever I find myself
Connected with the mysteries of life and find the light that
  shows me where my gift was coming from.
When I leave you, I feel empty because you are the part of me
  That stayed in one spot, where I can find
Myself in images of experiences in light.
It all begins with a white color and my hand touching you, try-
  ing to wake you up early in the morning with the first light of
  day…my loyal forever friend…fifty years of me and my easel
  in one spot.

Your Face

⌘

When I see your face, I see a vision of the happy past Passion and violet colors all over your eyes.
I try to catch your smile so I can steal it for myself just for a moment so I can enter your story of the past.
You speak with the voice of truth, still tracking the path of the carriage.
Your hands are so soft, and they carry the love of a sunflower. When I see your face, I see a vision of the happy past Passion and violet colors all over your eyes.
I want to know the color of your eyes…they are brown in one moment,
But then I see a touch of green covering your untouched tears, I want to know how you make love through passion
And the violet colors that see all over your eyes,
I touch your face and smile at the same time. I can feel the power of your world
When you speak through the voice of truth. I thank the sun for shining on you.
I thank the moon for guiding you at night. I thank the stars for being there for you.
I thank God for giving me you in my heart. When I touch your face I see the happy past
That I want to see…close your eyes, I want to kiss them with my passion and red colors that I carry for you.
I love you now and after this moment through my dreams and imagination.

I Was In Deep Sleep
⌘

There was a time I forgot how to cry. There was time I forgot how to love.
There was a time when I couldn't feel pain. I couldn't recognize the colors of spring. There was a time when I lost track of time. Forget the past, because a fog was hiding the future from my heart.
There was time I didn't know the difference between light and dark.
I forgot my dreams.
There was a time when I didn't know how to wonder about my life…where it was going to take me.
The next day of daylight,
There was a time I died while I was alive.
One morning, I felt the morning dew on my face.
From nowhere, a butterfly came and landed on my hand.
The same morning rain wet my hair, and I woke up from the deep sleep that held me under a spell of sadness. I looked around and couldn't recognize the world
that was around me.
I woke up and stood next to myself, reaching for my steps that I left a long time ago. I started smelling the fresh air
And the aroma of flowers that didn't bloom yet. I remembered how it felt
To be cold in the early hours of morning. I remembered to walk again on the street that I thought I got lost on.

I felt fire in me, looking to spread the flames of my soul.
Your words of promise woke me up. I was ready to let you be my shaper
And show me one more time why I was living. There was a time I was dead while I was alive, and you woke me up because I was your child.
You are my shaper now, and I want you to lead me forever. And if I get lost again, don't let me sleep too deep because I know now why I am here.
Thank you for watching over me, dear God.

Nobody
⌘

Nobody can know what one moment from another moment can turn into.
Nobody can see what is not told.
We can only hope for moments to come, but you can change everything.
From one thought that you can see, through our hope and faith.
Sometimes we push you away and replace you with earthly things we want to have.
But when you take that away,
We realize we can never know what one moment from another moment can turn into.
And we start hoping again for moments to happen. I watched tonight, every star in the sky
And wondered which one you are going to give me for my new start.
Only you can change things around our world. I understand that for the first time…tonight.

Don't Look Back

⌘

Don't ever look back on your past. You will be trapped inside the anger
That will turn your world under the spell of jealousy. Don't look back on your lost moments of life.
An old wish that you never finished
Is meant to be left alone…somebody else is going to finish it.
Don't ever look back on your past.
Light is always in front of you…try to reach for happy beginnings and new visions of your dreams. Search for the light in front of you if you want to see and feel the deep breath…in you is beauty. Don't ever look back on your past.
Let the light in front of you shine on your face. Warm your heart inside your hands.

Kaltrina Hoti

Hold My Hand

⌘

I am smiling and loving and wishing all at the same time
I want you to hold my hand because that is the only way you can understand what I feel in this moment.
I want you to smile and love and wish at the same time, just like I do…so hold my hand
And watch how we create a golden rainbow. I came from the deepest ocean,
Made my first steps on the sand
So deep, you could plant a rose of love.
I dreamed light and brought it in my reality vision. Hold my hand; I want to share this with you and them.
I am smiling and loving and wishing all at the same time.
I am living life through mountains and rivers blessed with rain, blessed with wind, blessed with fogs early in the morning.
Hold my hand, and let's walk over the golden rainbow.
Find your color to paint your story.

Because Of Mountains Days

⌘

I can take my time forever, thinking of my mountains days.
Ah,…fresh cold air in the mornings will make me think of
Him, make me think of my first love and kisses we wished to
 give to each other.
Because of cold air of the early morning, I learn to speak my
 thoughts.
I can take my time, forever thinking of my mountains days. The
 door of the old oven will make a strong noise
When I stoke the fire in the morning…I still can smell the
 wood burning.
Because of the morning flames from the old oven, I learned to
 listen to what my soul wants to teach me.
I can take my time, forever thinking of my mountains days. I
 used to go deep in the forest and look for dry branches
on the ground.
My grandmother used them to start the fire.
Because of the forest wind, I learned to sing together with birds.
 I can take my time, forever thinking of my mountains days.
I used to watch the rain and the lighting of the sky talking to
 each other.
Because of mountains, days I know the power of God. Because
 of my grandmother, I have days from mountains.

Saranda

⌘

When you wake up in the morning, I can't see your blue eyes.
When you wake up in the morning, I can't touch your face.
But I am there next to you,
Braiding your hair through the wind,
Wishing you a beautiful day through my faith. You are my first
　spring yellow flower
That I always look to see and have.
You are my first snow before Christmas comes. You are a part of
　my heart that I wish to touch.
You are a part of me that I carry all the time through every
　challenge in life…you are my girl.
When you wake up in the morning,
You may not hear my voice, but I am there. When you want to
　cry, I will brush your tears. When you reach for the power of
　God, I will be your strength inside the words of the prayer.
You are a part of me that I always have in my dreams.

Linda's Eyes

⌘

There is a light inside of your eyes…I can see it, my dear friend.
I want you to smile for me and show me the fire of life that you carried with you all these years.
You are a mirror of the strength, beauty, and love of God. Let the light shine from your eyes.
No tear should touch your face.
There is a light inside of your eyes when I looked at you. It was my friend, and I smiled for you…I was happy.
I was happy to see the flame of life, full of good memories bringing elegance to your face…you are a queen
Who holds her golden crown inside her heart. Take a deep breath, my friend, don't be afraid. You have a light inside of your eyes.
It is God holding you in His hand, looking at you through your soul that is so pure, like the light of his Son.

Grandpa, Tell Me A Story
⌘

Little boy said, "Grandpa, tell me a story."
And he leaned on his knee, looked up to his face, waiting to
   hear what Grandpa would say.
Grandpa smiled and put his hands on his little face and said,
"I'll tell you a story about a brave man who lived many years
   ago.
The day he was born, the skies opened up with a golden rainbow.
   His mom and dad loved him so much.
From the first moment, they knew he had a special gift given to
   him. When he was a little boy of the village,
He never fought or said a bad word.
When he became a young man, he helped everybody he met. He
   wiped tears from old women's faces.
He gave water to the thirsty soldier.
He helped the blind man to see light in the darkness. He shook
   hands with every stranger.
One day, he decided to leave his village
To find a big rock so he could build a house.
He met new friends and asked for help.
He was building on top of the rock, his new house.
But one day, one friend betrayed him for a bag of golden coins.
   The brave man didn't get mad; he forgave his friend.
He started walking through a dark forest.
In the beginning, he was scared, but he knew
At the end of the forest road, he would find his way back home.

His father was waiting for him with light in his hands
He had missed him so much…he took him in his arms again."
   The little boy smiled when he heard the brave man
Found his way home,
But in the eyes of the little boy there was one more question:
   "Grandpa…did the brave man go back to his friends
To see if they finished building his house?"
On Grandpa's face came a big grin, and he said, "They sent him a message…*the house is built.* Till this day, they still wait for him to come back."
The little boy jumped to his feet and said,
"I am happy they built his house. What was the name of the brave man?"
"My dear child, the brave man had many names; his true friends call him the Light of Life."

I Don't Want To Leave You

⌘

Time to say goodbye.
I am turning another page inside the light of my life.
One more time I will walk
Through this street to feel moments of the past. Maybe I will try to memorize that old tree on the side I used to come to on hot summer days
And count every wrinkle the tree has. One more time I will take a deep breath and speak to the flowers and birds.
I used to admire their beauty...
Maybe I will try to memorize songs and colors. They used to comfort me every time
I let my tears touch the ground. Time to say goodbye.
I am turning another page inside the light of my life.
One more time I will knock
On your door...slowly waking up every painting on the easel.
With my voice, I will fight my tears.
I can't leave you, but I have to say goodbye. You will be inside of me forever.
Why is it so hard to let you go, my friend? One more time, we will share our talk with morning coffee.
I am trying to fight my tears.
Don't call my name when I close the door. One more time I will look up at the blue sky and ask for a touch of rain to wash my face one more time on this spot.
Maybe I will be strong to call your name one more time. You

opened my mind and soul
For the power of God to enter.
You gave me the breath of pure, clean life. I am who I am right now
Because of you, my friend. I leave you my paintbrush
So you can remember that first painting of mine. I leave you my pencil on your desk
For you to remember all the wisdom— all the words we shared..
I can't leave you, but I have to say goodbye. Don't call my name when I close the door, my dear friend.

Kaltrina Hoti

Golden Coins Took My Friend
⌘

I am writing a letter to my friend, asking him,
Where did the loyalty of his, melt?
Golden coins can buy so much in our lives
And make friends that don't know our first names
Did he let his loyalty melt inside these coins?
I am writing a letter to my friend, asking him
What happened to him, to sell his first name?
I watched him growing as a young man,
Teaching him how to create solid steps in his first
Challenge of courage and love
Today he turned his head to the other side
When I needed him to stand up for my first name
I am writing a letter to my friend, asking him,
Does he remember his father's last wishes?
How much do you need to have to fulfill the hunger
Of your world?
A world of emptiness, full of golden coins
That will give him friends covered in the shadow of hate
One day he will write me back and ask for his
Memories back, but it will be too late
To ask for words that were given to him as a gift
I am writing a letter to my friend, asking him
To take my last words in his world, in peace with care

Beautiful Night

⌘

I love every moment of this night,
A quiet night full of peace and more peace.
The trees are in deep sleep, not one branch is moving.
As I looked far away I could see how night
Can be so full of light…light that is bright and shines.
I can still see the sky under a shadow of blue color.
Trees turn into a warm, gray touch.
The grass is golden from the moon's reflection.
It's a quiet night full of peace and more peace.
I know I am under many thoughts but they are all gone.
In this moment as I watch this night
Full of colors that are dancing around my eyes,
Only one thought comes in my mind—
To talk to God and tell Him how wonderful He is,
To show me a night like this.
I wanted in one moment to ask so many questions,
But I stopped.
I kept looking in the distance and admiring the night.
This peace answered all my questions.
I opened my heart to let this peace come inside of me.
Moments like this don't happen again.
I am leading my soul to become clean.
Come inside of me, become part of me.
The golden color is a symbol of God.
The blue color is a happiness of mine.
The gray is for wisdom in any challenges that life has for me.
Thank you, God, for this beautiful night
And the peace that becomes part of me.

He Dreamed

⌘

She was walking so light through the sands of the beach,
Wearing a long red dress
Her golden hair was covering her back
She looked like a falling star from the sky
From time to time, she would touch her hair
She had a smile on her face no man could buy
Every time I touched her hand I felt the power
Of life covered with love
I was scared to look in her eyes
The freedom of her soul was too strong for my heart
I wondered, *If I try to kiss her what will*
Become of this moment?
But I didn't touch her lips
I followed her steps through the sands of the beach
At the end of the beach there was a big rock
That the ocean will mark with big waves
She walked barefoot on the rock
'Til she reached the top and called me, by my name
She reached for my hand and said,
"Become part of me when I listen to the waves
Talking about arcane secrets."
Just before I touched her hand my dream disappeared
I was weak…but inside of me I can still see her
I decided to go to the beach and walk through the sand
Hoping she would leave the dream
I am waiting by the rock where waves
Talk about the ocean's secrets
I know she is coming…

I Wish I Had Stopped

⌘

I still remember his face, thick rings around the eyes
He used to sit on an old, green, rusty chair
By the corner of the store,
Watching people passing by and never saying a word.
When it rained he had umbrella. Even when it stormed, you
could find him in the corner of the store.
Nobody knew his name…
They called him Old Lonely Man.
He always had a yellow rose in his hand
So many times I wanted to go and sit by him
To hear the inside of his heart
People used to whisper different stories about him
Some believed he had lost the connection with reality
Some believed he was a brave solider and still lives
Through the fear of death
I believed he was waiting for the return of a lost love
That he carried in his soul
That morning I decided to share a moment
Of his life with my time…
I walked slowly by the corner of the store
The old, green, rusty chair was empty, and everything looked so
different
The yellow rose on the old, green, rusty green chair was thirsty
for water
Crying for the touch of the old lonely man
He was gone…
So many times I wanted to stop.
I missed his story…
Did I?

If You Let Me

I will slowly enter your shadow
With a whisper of my voice to cover your body
Reach for your hand and take you
To the world of fantasy.
I will reach for your heart to plant
Seeds of my love, and you will be happy
The moment I give you
The treasure of my thoughts.
I will slowly melt our bodies in a
Moment of blue color and you will
Turn into a flame of fire that never burns.
I will slowly enter your shadow
And become the moon and the sun at the same time.
Only then you will know
What love can bring in the world of fantasy.
I will become your water when you are thirsty
Only if you let me show you
The treasure of my thoughts that I carry for you...
If you only let me.

Word of God

⌘

Each of us is born with one word of God
In the beginning we can't write it or say it aloud
Time comes and we can see those four letters of
One word of God that is in us…
Life
Time comes, and we learn to say it out loud
Time comes, and we learn to write it
Time comes, and we start searching how to write it
Do we want all capital letters?
Do we want curves? What size do we want our four letters to be?
Before we know it, we start having our own ideas
How the word should be written
We start hiding behind the word and create shadows
That don't belong to us
We forget to give, and slowly, we are building
Walls around the word of God
Because of the shadow, the light is gone from
The first word of God that was given to us
Life means to live…to live means to think
Can we stop for one moment?
And think about every word we carry?
They are written somewhere already…
For one moment, can we replace anger with peace?
Can we replace jealousy with happiness for others?
The greediness of ours with giving from the heart?
For one moment, can we try to write
The one word of God that is in us…
Life?
The way is engraved in a big holy book
Can we do all this before the word *Life*
Is replaced with the word Emptiness in life?

Dean Smith

⌘

His name begins with cowboy stories, as his heroes
His name begins with the voice of the grandmother
That he can still hear
If that is what you want to do, go and try it
Life in wonders doesn't matter
His name begins with the shadow of our country
Bringing back a wining spirit…gold from the Olympics
His name begins with hope and faith
His name begins with challenges
He shows the world what cowboy spirit means
He shakes hands with many people around the world
But he never sold his soul
He believes in life; he believes in hope
He believes in words of wisdom
That he learned from his heroes
His name is part of real history
That can teach us never to step over routes of the past
That can teach us dreams come true if they are in us
Dean Smith…the name that shines through
   love, loyalty, and faith
Inside the light of life that God wants to have for all of us,
His wise word is so strong
Never sell your soul

New Beginning

⌘

I am strong,
I am Me
Sometimes when I get scared,
I think of life I want to reach
They say dreams come true
If we have them to dream

I am stronger,
I am Me
Waiting for the right time to come for me
And it will, I am waiting
I asked wisdom and faith to cover me
In times when I get attacked by fear

I am strong,
I am Me
My soul has seen
Tears and happiness at the same time
I am strong to be strong
I am waiting for my time

I am strong,
I am Me
Starting a new beginning that my dream is asking

I am strong,
I am Me
I am following the light of life to lead me

OldFriendship

⌘

Once we had friendship
Once we had a friendship full of laughs and moments
Once we use to shake hands, and today,
We build walls between us, not knowing why
I was hoping you would come out from your fears
But you didn't…
All I have left is to ask you,
"Can you look me in the eyes
When I forgive you the past?
Can you look for your truth when the time comes?
We all get challenged by unjustness
So we can know the difference
When we become thirsty for truth to take our side
I faced my unjustness and my truth was silent
I can't judge your actions…
The truth is my weapon
I will be silent
You can't judge what you see, but what you feel
What you feel is called truth
Truth is silent and strong when it enters inside of us
Can you look at me, strength in the eyes,
When I forgive you the past?
Can you stand up straight when your time comes
To search for your truth in moments of unjustness?
Can you look me in the eyes when I—"

I Asked God

⌘

Through memories of my life, I realize
Bitterness was inside of me
From all the challenges life gave me
In moments of wonder I felt…
And wanted bitterness to leave me
I turned my heart to Good and asked him to clean
My soul one more time
I closed my eyes and let the prayer take me
In a miracle moment of light
I felt peace all over my body
My heart started laughing the way I never did before,
And then tears dropped on my face
It was a feeling of peace and tears of happiness
At the same time
I felt lighter than a feather,
Stronger than a rock,
Bigger than a mountain,
Deeper than the sea,
Higher than the blue sky
I felt God giving me a new beginning
Life without bitterness
When I opened my eyes,
I was His child
Life is a gift from God. Live it with love.

Kaltrina Hoti

The Inside Of My Day

⌘

I love to wake up at the same time with the sun,
And watch how night goes to sleep,
And feel the first light of the day on my face.
In that moment I wish to paint
On a big canvas, a love story.
As I begin to mix the colors,
I can feel the happiness inside of me.
My brush starts to dance, and I follow her movement.
With a touch of precious red, a little bit of cobalt blue,
Following with ultramarine violet
My love story begins to come alive
On the big canvas of morning.
As the day goes deeper inside of the story,
I smile and bring king's blue to finish the love moment.
I love to wake up at the same time with sun
And paint on a big canvas.
First, though, I can find in the morning light
The sun, the canvas, and me.
This is the way I wish my day always to be.

Power Of Purple Color

⌘

You know me.
We met through your first breath.
Between us are clouds, oceans, and rivers.
Between us is time and thoughts.
We met…maybe…
You can't remember? But deep inside of you,
You know me.
Open your heart. I promised to be there for you.
First you need to remember the light that I gave you.
Open your heart; It's time for you to remember.
I will remind you again through light and darkness.
We need to exchange our thoughts again,
Before it is too late to take you away from the deep sleep of your soul.
Sometimes you hide the tears,
Trying to show fire in your eyes…thinking nothing can stop you.
Have mercy on yourself.
You wish to have that touch of rain.
You think you know which color is the sun?
Sometimes you take the world in your own hand.
Do you believe you can do that?
Give yourself love from the people that love you.
Take what your heart wants…sometimes you need help.
I was, I am, I will be understanding.
Your soul comes from me.
You are the gift that I created for somebody.
I am, I was, I will be…I will wait for you to remember me.

Kaltrina Hoti

True Word
⌘

A word is a weapon that targets the soul
It can make you carry heaviness on the chest
It will make you cry without tears
Or…
It will make you feel like a butterfly
And smell like the best flower that God creates

A word is a weapon that targets the soul,
And then it comes back to you
Because your mind is the nest of your soul
If somebody gives you heaviness
Let the word sleep in your mind…
A mind can break rocks
A mind can put mountains together

Choose to feel free
Forgiveness for others is your power to fly
High in the sky and overlook the soul and mind
Choose to speak true words and bring love around you
Moments of truth live forever inside of true words

Did You Remember?

⌘

You let the wind play with your hair.
Did you ever say thank you for that?

The rain brings so much around you.
If you like, it will wash your face.
Did you ever say thank you for that?

You breathe air for the next breath of life.
Did you ever say thank you for that?

Your hands are full of dirt…
Today you can plant a flower, tomorrow you can bring bread
   through the dirt in your hands.
Did you think of saying thank you for that?

Every day the river is in you…
The waterfall of life is everywhere.
Without the breath, the dirt, the wind, and the water you can't
   live your destiny.

I am thanking for me, I am thanking for you.

Our Melody

⌘

On the branches of the tree, a symphony plays.
Every bird I ever saw is here today.
Music of their songs is replacing the thoughts of wonder.
The day of a new beginning is happening now.
It's peace in our soul…
The stumbling moment is gone…
My poem becomes musical note that lead a symphony of light.
A moment in life happens through things we think we know.
If you can separate them in silence,
Past wishes disappear, and the light of truth will lead you.
You will walk with forgiveness and vision of hope.
The inside gift of your soul becomes your life.
On the branches of the tree a symphony plays.
Everybody can hear our melody.

Panorama Of Studio

⌘

An old wooden fence is leaning on the rock,
Talking to each other about the past
The rock is leaning on the fence
The fence is leaning on the rock
By their side, an old rock wall
Is covered in blue color,
Blue color from the canvas on the wall,
Blue color paint through the eyes of a child,
Blue color of smiles
In between them, one rose is whispering,
Always stay green, but never grow more.
Two words are said…nobody will ever know
When the sun dries the ground, one spot is always wet…
The tears of mystery drop. They always will stay there.
The fence is leaning on the rock
The rock is leaning on the fence

What Happened?
⌘

I remember the days growing up.
Your freckles used to make me laugh.
I remember days growing up.
I loved your face in tears; I loved your face in wonders.
I remember the growing up days.
You took everything away. You erased the book of your life.
I can see melting words that you shared with love once.
All the stories with me are gone…you took what was not
   yours.
They called me through the voice of pain…
"He's gone. He took his life away."
Will you every sleep again? Will you ever wonder again?
No! You will not…
   my brother, memories are gone…
Life is a treasure. You did not understand.
How are we supposed to remember life that erases?

Butterfly

⌘

It was a red color, with a touch of gold.
She was slowly coming to me.

In one moment, I saw only gold, and it reminded me of the
 morning sunrise,
Reminded me of an autumn kiss on the ground
That turns everything into gold.

In one moment, I saw only red, and it reminded me of
The sky before it goes to sleep,
Reminded me of his lips that I wish to kiss.

It was red and gold color put together on velvet.
She was slowly coming to me and I watched and wondered,
When is it going to disappear?
How many can say…
I saw a butterfly slowly coming to me,
Giving me the pleasure of her colors
And her magic moment.

Kaltrina Hoti

Moment
⌘

It was like never before.
Trees opened their branches and stayed still.
Every flower was giving me the best colors.
The air was still and at the same time talking to me.
Through the beauty of nature, I felt the moment of silence
Everything was moving and quiet at the same time.
I was in between the rain and the wind that only I could see…
I felt the moment of the day, a silent day…a day of peace…
I saw every beauty of the day through my heart.
I touched that beauty with my eyes.
I touched the silence of the day.
Will I ever be the same?
It's different today…I hear birds singing my song!
A red rose is hidden in my eyes…
A rock is connected with a green pasture.
The wind is hugging the sun while clouds are calling for rain.
   It's different today…
I am standing on the rock, watching the river from the rain
   drops.
Time is timed through His hands.
Life is coming slowly through the rainbow.
I wish to be one of the colors that shines through His hands.
It's different today…
The wind braided my hair, whispered inside of me.

Stolen Moment

I tried to separate reality
From the feeling that you gave me so it would last forever.
I was in the moment of fantasy, a beautiful dream,
But I knew it would be time to wake up.
Your eyes tried to tell me something.
I was weak at that moment.
Your words took me with you. I did not want to fight back.
It felt so warm, but I knew
I couldn't be touched by your fantasy...
The eyes of the stranger stole the moment from me,
Left me with a wondering dream
In between the time that is coming
And the time I will always try to change,
With my imagination and unloved love, for him.

After The Rain

⌘

Each day I believe and I hope I am getting closer to my dream.
Whatever the day gives me, I take it with smile and a vision that I carry inside.
I was once in the world where I lived only from the outside of me.
I lived to keep somebody else's dream shining, not knowing why.
People knew me because of what I had. Gold, silver, and silk were a bridge between us.
It almost drowned my soul, created another of me that I did not like at all.
I became a stranger to myself and a perfect picture for others.
But now is different.

Each day I believe and hope I am getting closer to my dream.
Every living moment is me. I feel peace, and my soul balloons to me.
Gold and silver are replaced with dreams and hopeful words for others.
Slowly I am becoming part of the rainbow colors after rain,
Giving to the moon and sun part of my story that is waiting for the blue sky.
Full life is lived when you can read your name in the stars. I am crossing over the rainbow. The rain stopped.
My first star is shining on my steps. Once I lived from outside of me.
Now I live inside of every giving moment, dreaming, hoping to touch
The vision inside my heart…it mixes a royal blue color with red and light yellow sunshine.

I Miss My Father

⌘

Today, you are reaching for the light,
Wondering what is going to be on the other side.
Today you will find answers you searched for all your life,
And I am giving you my last tear with the thirst of your words and love.
I can see your face in between my dreams, and in the first moment of the morning light.
Today you are seeing the other side while I am wondering,
Can you see me now?
I wonder,
Will you wish to come in my dreams and tell unspoken words to me?
I wonder,
Do you have regrets in my words and your tears?
I know you hide one tear for me deep inside of you
So the world won't see your love for me.
I wonder,
Do you wish right now to tell me I love you, my child?
Today you are inside the light and I am wishing you can see me through the blue sky,
Trying to touch my face and telling me,
Don't cry.
Deep in me I can read your words. I know now love is free.
I forgive you for every moment you won't be with me.
My love for you will shine through the light you stand in right now.
Thank you for the words. I try to live them through.
I give you my love inside your peace.
I am going to miss you, dear father.

Dream

⌘

I wonder what our dreams are supposed to be.
What do they mean? In our reality, our living moments
Sometimes we remember them, and sometime we don't.
Some of them make us happy, some make us cry.
Last night, I dreamed of my childhood
Coming through a water spring, full of bubbles,
And every bubble had one picture of the past.
I was there trying to choose what to remember.
Is it real, to feel what you see in the dream?
Is it real, to feel the dream inside the living moment?
From time to time we forget life that we lived
Because we want to be get connected with the real dream.
So what is the dream?
Separating from a living moment by choice,
Or choosing to dream through our hearts and minds?
Times are changing, and we don't know
What dreams are supposed to be for us.

Tattooed Face

You are angry at the outside world
That you created, not knowing why
You forgot to open the doors of your mind and power
You're scared there is nothing left there
Sour words and rainbows are over you, with a dark cloud
Replacing the real you
You want to be different from others
But you all look the same
Tattoos and chains around your neck
You pushed your gifts away,
Trying to use the shadows of others as your tools
Wake up, my friend…
There is so much you want to say
I can see your unspoken words when you are looking
From the corner, behind the tree, from below your niche
I will not judge you.
I am supposed to give you a hand
If you are a leader don't look like the rest of them
If you are a follower, follow the light, not darkness
I can hear unspoken words coming from you
Look me in the eyes. You may see sparkly light
That belongs to you
Wake, my friend, I will not judge you

Kaltrina Hoti

Over The Rainbow
⌘

It pulls your heart from feelings
That you try to understand
You become thirsty for the past memories
That remind you of home
And where, for the first time, you understood
The feelings of love and hope

It pulls your heart and it hurts,
But you can't feel the pain
You become pain itself,
Wondering,
What is going on? Where do I start? Where do I stop?
How do I come out from this fire circle
And be again a peaceful sunflower trying
To follow the light of life with a smile?

It pulls your heart from you
It pulls you from the dreams
You have to fight for the words you choose
To keep in the heart, to survive
You have to look at your face in the mirror and see
Who is waiting in the outside world of yours,
Trying to reach for your feelings and touch.
It is so scary to be in middle of an unknown crowd,
Letting the true colors of life shine through your
   eyes and hands,
But it's the only way to cross over the rainbow of a dream
To dream takes more than courage, opening the doors
   for new beginnings
You need faith and more faith, and hope and love for life and
   the light
So close your eyes and take your hope and faith
That you carry for life and light to take you away

From the firing circle, so you can cross over the rainbow of your dream
You can do it, my friend

For The First Time

⌘

I can still see the look of your eyes
It will be inside of my heart forever
So beautiful, they made me smile
And wished to be loved by them
For the first time, I wanted to put a spell on time
And make everything around us freeze
Everything except us, me and you
So our eyes could make love
Through this magic moment
I can still see the look of your eyes
So bright, one sparkling light in the center
They just shook my heart, and I was scared for a second
How much power was in them?
For the first time, emotion stole my heart
Your lips became mine
My body was melting inside your shadow
I was wondering,
Do you feel the same?

My Brush

⌘

My brush is dancing through colors on a canvas,
Painting memories that don't want to remember me anymore.
Everything comes and goes in our lives, in people with messages.
My brush is dancing through colors on a canvas,
Painting you in my past…
Painting me coming back in your life,
And you will never know what it will be…
As wind, maybe rain.
You will never know.

My brush is dancing through colors on a canvas,
Creating love of life and memories of the future,
Painting you turning your head away from me.
Today, you don't want to know me,
But my brush knows you forever.
That one moment is living inside of your portrait,
And the artist is my brush.
Dancing with your color on my canvas,
Painting memories that don't want to remember me anymore

In The Red Book

⌘

You built the walls and called my house.
Inside, you tried to paint my image.
Do I look like that?
You invited me to come and see you.
What do you want me to see?
My words are spoken in the red book.

I can hear your voice all the time.
You can see me only through your own eyes.
You tried to talk to me between the walls
In more than one way…and I wonder,
Why?
I don't need to be divided in any way.
Learn forgiveness. Touch the hand that needs you.
Give the child bread…learn to love things that you have.
Learn to see me through your own eyes…
I am everywhere you are.
My words are spoken in the red book.

You can take a breath next to the first spring flower.
Your imagination can go over yourself.
You are creating your own world…how far do you want to go?
You let your father's well go dry. Your mother's words are
   fading. Your roots are getting dry…stop.
Remember this is passing time.
How far do you want to go?
Are you going to stop challenging with your own blood?
I am asking you, through my rain, fire, wind, and words.
You are creating your own world inside my hand.
I am watching, waiting for you to wake up…
How far do I let you go?
I am everywhere you are.

www.ingramcontent.com/pod-product-compliance
Lightning Source LLC
Chambersburg PA
CBHW021157080526
44588CB00008B/383